Bread
and
Butter

Bread and Butter

Poems of the Spirit

JEAN R. MORE

ARPress
ILLUMINATING IDEAS
EMPOWERING VOICES

ARPress
45 Dan Road Suite 5
Canton MA 02021

Hotline: 1(888) 821-0229
Fax: 1(508) 545-7580

Ordering Information:

Quantity sales. Special discounts are available on quantity purchases by corporations, associations, and others. For details, contact the publisher at the address above.
Printed in the United States of America.

ISBN-13:   Paperback   979-8-89356-104-3
                eBook   979-8-89356-129-6

Library of Congress Control Number: 2024902495

CONTENTS

CHILDREN

Children, The Ultimate Treasure. 2

Dear Brother 3

Dear Sister 4

My Son, An Eagle Scout. 5

Our Own 6

Sing His Songs of Praise. 7

What is the Worth?. 8

CHOICES

A Commitment. 12

An Open Invitation 14

Attain Unto In This Life 15

Attitude Makes the Difference. 16

Daily Interview 17

Endure To The End 18

Linger In The Mind. 19

Live For Eternity. 20

Only Two Treasures Rise In The End 21

Only 22

Opposition 23

Purity of Thought 24

Recognize 25

Recorded In Heaven 26

Run And Not Be Weary 27

Word of Knowledge 28

DEATH

A Tribute To My Angel Mother 30

Back Home At Last 31

Help Me Understand. 32

I Too Have Suffered There. 33

EXAMPLE

Be Humble And Meek 36

Choose Wisely Your Example 37

Example Through Eternity. 38

Handicapped 39

January Blahs, I Challenge You 40

Stand Forth And Be Counted 41

The Standards We Live 42

FAITH

Added Upon 44

Councils; A Heavenly Pattern 46

Creations of God. 47

God Bless You Precious Friend 48

Missionary Prayer 50

Prayer of Hope. 52

The Blessing of Faith 53

To Each Of us 54

Trust In God 55

FAMILIES

Eternal Families 58

Families Are Eternal 59

Family Circle 60

Fifty Years Is Not Enough 61

Ordained Of God. 62

Missionary Brother 63

Precepts Everlasting 64

Strengthening Our Families 65

The Rising Generation 66

GOALS

A Petition 68

An Equalizing Gift 69

Be Creative and Frugal 70

Buy The Temporal Lamp First 71

Climb High 72

Desire Is The Key 73

Don't Let Him Down 74

Goals Forever 75

Goals Of Youth 76

Just Yesterday 77

Life 78

Of One Heart and Mind 79

Search and Gain Wisdom 80

So Temporary 81

GOSPEL

Abide In Hope And Prayer 84

The Book Of Mormon: Beacon For Our Day . . . 85

Consider Your Debt 86

Empire Stone Rolling Forth 87

Eternal Vow 88

Greater Love 89

His Holy House 90

Is There A Place?. 91

Israel 92

Lord's Time 93

My Divine Nature 94

My Garden 95

No More Strangers. 96

Priesthood… A Gift To All. 97

Sonnet 2/73 98

Steeples of Glory. 99

The Sweet Gift Of Prophecy. 100

The Gift 101

To Be Without Guile 102

What Of The Godhead 103

When I am Humble 104

Worth The Gain 105

GRATITUDE

A Sacred Gift. 109

Before The World Was… Remember?. 110

Gratitude 112

Happiness 113

More Gratitude Give Me. 114

Rainbows In The Rain 115

Thankful Heart. 116

The Debt 117

JESUS CHRIST

    Bridges. 120

    Be Mine 121

    Eastern Morn, What A Glorious Day 122

    In The Image Of God 123

    In Tune. 124

    Just By Chance? 125

    Let Us Seek Light 126

    Not Merely A Man. 127

    One of the least of these 128

    Our Faith In Christ Will See Us Through 129

    Son Rise 130

    Sonnet 4-73 131

    Supper Of Remembrance 132

LOVE

    Eternal Vow 134

    Friendship is a Circle 135

    In All Things, It is Shown 136

    Language Of the Soul 137

    Love My Son. 138

    Love 139

    Those Who Have Learned 140

    Timeless Magic 141

    Told and Retold 142

NATURE

    Chariot Wings 145

    Cotton In The Sky 146

    Frozen Crystals 148

Golden Splendor 149

I Love The Rain 150

I Would Like To Remember 151

Mighty Sea 152

Promised 153

Radiant Sun 154

Roses 155

Rushing Diamonds 156

Sunset 158

Tall And Grand 159

Winter Whispers 160

OBEDIENCE

Be Ye Prepared 162

Called It Blest 163

Covenant Blessings 164

Honestly... Just That Little Thing... 165

Maybe It's Near 166

More Purity Give Me 167

Much Is Required 168

Obedience 169

Practicing Holiness 170

Purity Of Thought And Deed 171

The Loser 172

The Purpose Of Life 173

The Reason Because 174

Trimming Our Lamp 175

PARENTS

    But I Do 178

    Dear Dad 179

    I Remember 180

    Mother, Kind And Dear 181

    There Is A Time 182

RELIEF SOCIETY

    Called Relief Society 184

    Charity Never Faileth 185

    Charity 186

    Discipleship Through Service 187

    Not Just A Number 188

    Rejoice In The Organization Of R.S. 189

    Take Note 190

    The Purpose And Plan 191

    Watching Over Each other 192

    We Are Sisters In One Family 193

REPENTANCE AND REVELATION

    Be Born Again 196

    Prepare To Receive Revelation 197

    Remorse and Repentance 198

    That I May Heal You 199

    The Stillness 200

SERVICE AND TALENTS

    A Missionary 202

    An Instrument In The Hand Of God 203

    In The Service Of 204

Misused 205

Service 206

Spreading Seeds 207

The Arts 208

The Earth Is The Lord's 209

Weak Indeed 210

Ye Have Done It Unto Me 211

Your Sleep Is No More 212

TRIALS

A Walk Among Flowers 215

And I Wept 216

I Am Not Troubled 218

I Can Only See Yesterday 219

I Need Not Fear 220

I Wish I Had All The Answers 221

More Meekness In Trial 222

Peace Be With You 223

CHILDREN

CHILDREN, THE ULTIMATE TREASURE

By Jean Moore 7-2016

In this world of experience, we have many choices,
And we hear the persuasion of a great many voices.
Rearing sons and daughters is an option of late
That has been forgotten, discarded, or just second rate!

This commandment from God has been pushed aside,
In favor of travel and leisure or building our pride.
Our potential for Parenthood is a calling from God,
Not just a pastime, a hobby or job.

Our Ultimate Treasure on earth or above.
Are the Children we nurture and care for in love.

DEAR BROTHER

By Jean R. Moore 1968-9?

It's your birthday today what can I do?
I guess I will just say,
That I Love You.

I am sure glad you happen to be my brother,
I would not want to trade
You for another.

You have been a good brother
All through the season,
I will just have to take,
Your terrible teasing!

Now on your birthday I hope you're content,
To make you that way
This letter I've sent.

I hope you are glad and enjoy the whole day,
May every good thing
Happen your way.

Enjoy it today, while today is still here.
It won't come again
For another whole year.

I wish I could write the words of my heart,
But of course, this is only:
A very small part!

DEAR SISTER

By Jean R. Moore 1969

Upon this very special day
There is something good, I'd like to say.
I've rarely said that I love you,
But I hope you know I really do!

You have been good all through the years,
And have not caused too many tears.
Sometimes you help me with my cares,
And keep from me, sheer despair.

Now upon this special day
May every good wish come your way.
You are now 20 in a great big world,
To you…her treasures, she has unfurled.

Twenty years ago, when you were born,
I'm sure our mom had a happy morn.
Through the years, you grew tall,
Mom was careful that you didn't fall.

Have a lovely, happy day,
Keep God in mind, and you won't stray.
Life is happy, good and kind,
I'm sure her pleasures, you will find.

MY SON, AN EAGLE SCOUT

By Jean R. Moore
(January 6, 2008)

As the changing seasons come and go,
I watched my son,
Develop and grow.
I remember how in days gone by
I would see him learn,
Experience, and try.

At first, as a cub:
Carving wood, racing cars,
Building fires, mapping stars.
Developing friendship,
Learning to trust.
Working together,
Or alone
If he must

Hundreds of miles
By bike, or on foot.
He has logged with experiences,
As values take root.

At times, when he stumbled,
I would have rushed to give aid,
But the challenge was his,
To walk tall; unafraid.

On the breath of the wind
He is now soaring high.
With skills he has earned
He is ready to fly,

Like an eagle of strength
Your path is well done.
Walk tall and do good
For you are my son!

5

OUR OWN

By Jean Moore

If mother is
the heart
and warmth
of every home…..

Then surely baby
is
the very
fiber of love,
and most lasting
of what we call…

OUR OWN!

SING HIS SONGS OF PRAISE

By Jean R. Moore

Said the child to his mother
As he sat upon her knee;
You say Heavenly Father loves me
But how can I be sure...
That He's aware of me?

Then quoted she, a primary song;
A favorite from her youth...

The child gazed up into her smile,
And asked with wondering eyes:
Then how can I show love for Him
Who dwells in yonder skies?

She answered simply, several ways. . .
Just Sing His Songs of Praise.

WHAT IS THE WORTH?

By Jean R. Moore

What is the price, placed on a child?
What is the value of guiding their soul?
Is there profit in caring? Is there reason to share?
Are they worth all the trouble, and heartache and prayer?

To understand the price of a child
and recognize the worth of their soul;
Let us imagine the family is yours
Your sons and daughters, and their lifetime scores.

They have gone off to school in a place far away,
you can not be there to help them along.
They must choose for themselves
Between right and wrong.

Some have been faithful for keeping in touch.
And some have gained wisdom, and knowledge and such.
Would you not want them to share what they've learned?
To be leaders and teachers, in the knowledge they've earned?

Would you not want them to guide and persuade,
To love one another, with talents unstayed?
And would you not bless them in measures untold;
With the treasures of life, and gifts. . .hundred fold!

So it is with our Father above, this life is but a school.
He loves each child, for each is His own.
And each has come from His Heavenly Home.
And so again I ask these thoughts;

What is the price, placed on a child?
What is the value of guiding their soul?
Is there profit in caring? Is there reason to share?
Are they worth all the trouble, and heartache and prayer?

Doctrine & Covenants 18:10

CHOICES

A COMMITMENT

By Jean R. Moore
RS conference (1986?)

A discussion I heard, now many years past,
Between two friends, who traveled along.
I have returned to this very path
To see what resolves have guided their song.

Said one to the other, as they spoke years ago…
Let us resolve, to plan and commit,
To serve and be served,
As good life will permit.

Oh, said the other; you can of course,
But as for my life, I see not the need.
I require no plan to keep me a float,
I'll take what I get, and surely succeed.

So their paths parted and each went his way
To various fancies, both grand and small.
The one had a plan, a commitment and goal;
The other had naught, and no plan at all.

The one with a goal had struggles and pain;
His commitment was firm, so he had to remain.
But because he was sure of the goals in his life,
He won great respect, and life was his claim.

But to the other; he fared not so well,
With no plan in life, no purpose, no goal;
He cared not a trifle to win or to lose,
But wandered the highway…..a destitute soul.

So all the years have come and gone,
And we all have fancies, both grand and small.
Some have a plan, a commitment and goal,
And others have naught, and no plan at all!

AN OPEN INVITATION

By Jean Moore

If we will have the treasure,
We must surely pay the price;
and spend our skill in learning truth
and not on rolling dice.

It's an open invitation
to search, to grow, to climb;
For learning is a journey,
or a process, etched in time.

To fill our minds and hearts and homes,
With wisdom, skill and light,
Is choosing life and liberty
Over idle waste and spite.

Truly there is open wealth, a kaleidoscope and more;
For knowledge is the key of hope. . . and skill, the open door.

ATTAIN UNTO IN THIS LIFE

By Jean Moore

So much of our time in this life is ill spent;
gathering objects and "stuff," to make us content.
And while we must do, enough to take care;
We can't take it with us to heaven up there.

More important than "stuff" or things we might buy
is the knowledge and wisdom, we take when we die.
We are commanded to teach one another
Learn wisdom and truth; and share with each other.

Learn of the heavens and things in the earth,
of nations and kingdoms; of science and birth.
Things that are now, by heaven's decree;
Things which have been or shortly must be.

Whatever knowledge and learning we gain
will rise with our soul and in memory remain.
So spend your time wisely, seek treasures of mind;
For knowledge and wisdom are surely divine!

ATTITUDE MAKES THE DIFFERENCE

By Jean R. Moore (High School)

Attitude makes all the difference,
of a pleasant day, and things going swell,
or a darkened road and grief all the way;
. . .but Attitude, makes the difference.

You can be like a rock, lying bare in the sand.
Leaving loneliness and hurt
Because you didn't understand.
Letting attitude get in the way of your joy,
Leaving tears and remorse,
As your empty ploy.
It can be like this, because it's your own choice,
. . .but Attitude, makes the difference.

Or you can be like gold, in a clear mountain stream,
Sharing your spirit, to reflect in the sun.
Letting attitude help
your soul through this world, leaving joy and great pleasure
through the spirit you hold.
It could be like this too,
Because it's your own choice,
. . .but Attitude, makes the difference.

So as you can see, and might have well noticed,
your own bad days,
when things are all wrong,
and the great days in life,
when things are just swell,
could point back to you,
in one small phrase,
. . .ATTITUDE,
MAKES THE DIFFERENCE

DAILY INTERVIEW

By Jean R. Moore

Have you kept your appointment
Every day;
To search the Iron rod,
In quiet thought
In an interview with God?

For He has said
To search His word,
To ponder and pursue;
He is always there for the interview
Waiting, loving,
How about you?

ENDURE TO THE END

By Jean R. Moore

Endure to the end my faithful one,
Keep courage and valor,
Till the setting of sun.

It won't be long now,
The time has gone fast,

Yes, time passes quickly,
When you view the far past.

But the end is not yet,
Though the world seems dark,

There still lies within you,
A strong, glowing spark.

Yes, time has now fled,
From the clutches of sin,

And the gates of your God,
Can enclose you within.

Yet the clock will not stop,
Through the eons of time,

But only move slower,
As the ladder we climb.

LINGER IN THE MIND. . .

By Jean R. Moore

The whisper of a melody
Will linger in the mind.
And when the LORD
Shall part
The curtain of
your heart. . .
what mel-o-dy
shall He find?

LIVE FOR ETERNITY

By Jean R. Moore

When the spiritual veil is drawn
Across our mortal mind;
And we forget our first estate
And the life we left behind
We must try to remember
When we're born on earth
The feelings of our spirit
Before our mortal birth.

We must live for eternity;
Earth is but a school.
We must listen to the spirit speak,
To give our soul renewal

We must walk by faith and love,
And let our spirit shine;
We must listen to the still small voice
Whose counsel is divine.
Remember all the promises,
The things we said we'd do;
The blessings that will come to us
If we are always true.

We must live for eternity
Earth is but a school.
We must listen to the spirit speak,
To give our soul renewal.

ONLY TWO TREASURES RISE IN THE END

By Jean Moore 9-5-1991

Only two treasures will rise in the end;

Our KNOWLEDGE attained,

And RELATIONSHIPS gained.

So build in your family a love that is sure,

Seek wisdom and truth, for these shall endure.

Only two treasures. . .

ONLY

By Jean R. Moore

Rainbows are never captured;
...only enjoyed.
Love is never taken;
...only shared
Endurance is never given,
...only earned;
Friendship is never found;
...only created.
Gratitude is never built;
...only felt.

OPPOSITION

By Jean Moore
(6/3/03)

In life there are trials
And there will be pain
But the struggles of life
Are as refreshing as rain.

If we are prepared
And if we are taught. . .
Then despite opposition
We shall not be caught!

PURITY OF THOUGHT

By Jean R. Moore

Thoughts and Ocean Waves. . .
They are
So much alike;
For like the pounding ocean waves
Eroding
Sand and shore.
Our thoughts erode our character
Unless
We keep them pure!

RECOGNIZE

By Jean R. Moore

Treasure the past:
The memories,
And friends.
Have faith in whatever
The future
Sends.
Keep a song
In your heart,
And a smile
In your eyes:
Happiness is free
If we But only Recognize!

RECORDED IN HEAVEN

By Jean Moore

Do you know the importance
of this special day?
Aware of the angels
who have paused in their way?

For the date of your baptism
And your choices in strife,
Are recorded in Heaven
in the
LAMB'S Book of Life.

RUN AND NOT BE WEARY

By Jean R. Moore
(High School)

There are laws that we must keep
Or in trouble we'll be deep.
The Word of Wisdom is one command,
That all should keep in every land.

Ye shall run and not be weary, and shall walk and not faint.
Such a promise is given to all of His Saints.

So let it rule you every day,
Don't let temptation make you sway.
You'll be strong in body and mind,
And the treasures of life you surely will find.

Make a choice, but make it here,
Don't ever wait till enticement is near.
You will always be happy; you will always be strong,
You will always be singing a cheerful song!

WORD OF KNOWLEDGE

By Jean R. Moore 7-97

We live in an age
When knowledge and power
Are given so freely
And increase every hour.

So by our own choice
We learn to love or disdain;
Gain wisdom or folly
..win peace or pain.

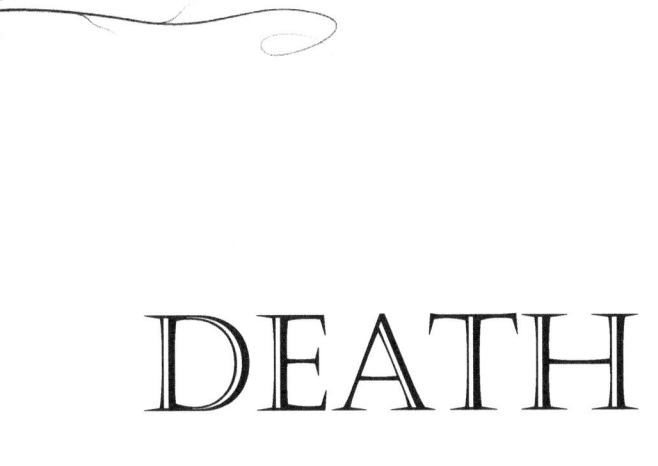

DEATH

A TRIBUTE TO MY ANGEL MOTHER

By Jean Moore 11-21-09

It's hard for me to realize, that Mom has really gone.
Her spirit lives with others now,
In splendor like the dawn.

I will miss her wisdom, her love and smiling face,
But I know that she is surely now
In a far more glorious place.

She could always make me feel better
No matter how deep the pain.
She often saw a brighter side,
Finding rainbows in the rain.

We have worked together, played together,
Prayed together,
Laughed and wept together too.
I am grateful for her life,
and testimony of all that's true.
All the memories come flooding back,
As fresh as morning dew.

She taught us to cook, to sew, and to sing;
She said, Look for the good in everything!
We shared so much of life and time,
So many thoughts and love sublime.
Sensitive to the needs of each other,
She was always quick to serve another;

This is a tribute to
My Angel Mother!

BACK HOME AT LAST

By Jean R. Moore 4-98

Life is a journey of joy and pain,
of success, disappointment,
sunshine, and rain.

When at last our journey's completed,
the experience gained
and sin is defeated,

Then we will pass through the veil of death,
leaving family and loved ones
of the parting…bereft.

But the sorrow is short, when faith is so strong,
for we know that the parting
will not be for long.

Impatiently waiting… like the splendor of dawn
reunion with loved ones
for those who pass on.

Be not grieved, nor remorseful of heart;
Rejoice and be glad,
Just remember the good part.

Yes, life is a journey and when it has passed,
Rejoice in the journey;
Back Home at Last

HELP ME UNDERSTAND

By Jean R. Moore
(for Karen Kadar)

Oh Father up in heaven, help me understand;
Help me bear the pain dear Lord, and calm my shaking hand.

For you see dear Lord, I loved this man, and deep within my heart,
I had a special tender place; our love we did impart.

For while he walked upon this earth, and trod the trail of life;
I felt a special spirit then, amid my toil and strife.

I loved him God so very much; my heart is torn in two;
For you see dear Lord, I know he's happy, living there with You.

But I miss him every passing hour; I miss his love and care;
I loved him Lord with all my heart, and now I feel despair.

So sooth my aching heart dear Lord, and wipe away my tears;
Give me strength to carry on, and take away my fears.

For now my love is gone from me, He's come to live with thee;
But I'll still miss his spirit Lord, until I touch eternity,

Perhaps someday we'll meet again, and speak words face to face,
And we shall live and love once more, protected my Thy grace.

Oh Father up in heaven, help me understand;
Help me bear the pain dear Lord, and calm my shaking hand.

I TOO HAVE SUFFERED THERE

BY Jean R. Moore

I offered up a prayer today, and in between my cries,
I asked the LORD to strengthen me and help me realize.
"Why," said I, "did he have to go?
Why did he have to die?"
Perhaps he was meant to return to Thee
In Thy celestial home on high."
Then I stopped and …listening, I thought I heard Him say…

"It was time for him to leave this earthly stage of clay.
My child, my child, listen to me there
For I have come to comfort thee,
In answer to thy prayer.
I have loved, as you have loved,
for one whom I have made;
For I was there and watched my Son,
As He wept in the Garden shade.
I heard His cry unto His God, but nothing could I do;
For through His love and sacrifice,
He saved your brother and you.
I saw Him as He suffered there, bleeding at every pore;
I saw Him give His mortal life, and open the eternal door.
Mortality is but a stage, in which all play a part.
But all too soon the part is done
and memories fill your heart.
My child, be wise in judgment now
…for I understand your grief;
Yes, I have suffered just as you, in the valley of no relief."
And as I knelt there pondering, reflecting on my prayer,
I seemed to hear the words repeat;
"I too have suffered there."

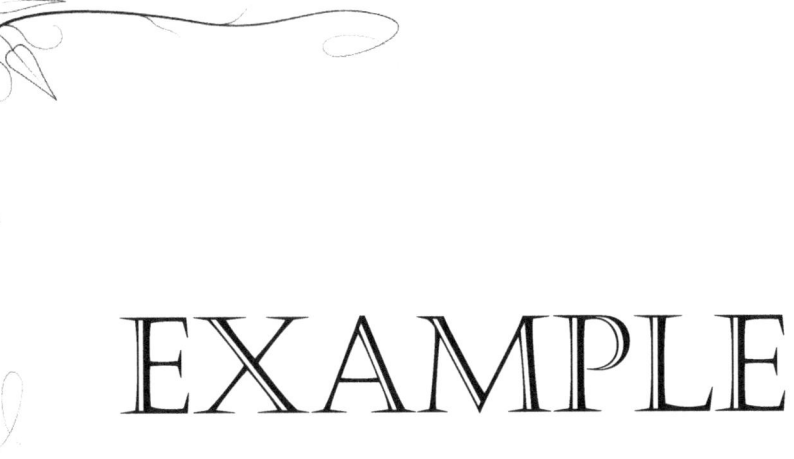

EXAMPLE

BE HUMBLE AND MEEK

By Jean Moore 8-2015

Following Jesus is not such a task;
If we choose His example,
and do as He asks.
His message to us, to be humble and meek,
is not a command
to be timid or weak.
But rather it is power to serve and be blest,
to have peace, hope and love,
and to meet every test.
To be humble and meek is a power so strong,
it will lift us to God,
where we hope to belong.

CHOOSE WISELY YOUR EXAMPLE

By Jean Moore 3-21-86

Choose wisely your example
And be careful of your guide;
Be certain of his character, before you follow stride.

Have you ever heard the story?
Of the eagle and the chicken;
Of how the eagle in the barnyard went a hopping and a'pickin.

The eagle really thought
That he was one of them
And he followed their example in the confines of the pen.

Then one day a naturalist
Saw the eagle in the yard
And he took him to a mountain top
where his flight could not be barred.

At first the eagle could not fly
For he had never tried before,
But then he saw between the clouds an eagle that could soar.

He spread his mighty wings aloft
And stretched toward the sun;
By matching flight with higher goals his freedom had been won.

And so it is with each of us,
We must wisely choose our guide
And be certain of his character before we follow stride.

For many of the valiant ones
Have been led too far astray
By choosing false examples and bending to their way.

For we were born as gods,
and our destiny is high
But we must rise, and set the course,
 to His glory in the sky.

EXAMPLE THROUGH ETERNITY

By Jean R. Moore (1971-2)

A chosen friend unto the LORD
Is seen in the apostle Paul,
For surely he was meant to be
An example through eternity.

This man called Paul was great indeed.
As a missionary to God's plan,
After the seed was truly conceived
The Gospel of CHRIST was gladly received.

Paul shared this gift, the Gospel light of Christ
To the people who would hear.
He taught eternal paradise
Through the LORD'S atoning sacrifice.

And unto us of Latter Days
The rules are still the same,
That we mush share the Gospel way
To those who've gone astray.

HANDICAPPED

By Jean R. Moore

If I could run and play,
Like other girls and boys
I'd play until the day was done,
With all my friends and toys.

If I could see the popcorn clouds
A dancing in the sky
I'd watch them frolic all day long,
A gliding like a butterfly.

If I could hear the robin's song
And smell the breath of spring
I'd listen to the sounds of love,
Which speak of God in everything.

JANUARY BLAHS, I CHALLENGE YOU

By Jean R. Moore

I challenge you,
Said my whispering soul,
To be happy for a day,
Not just, I'm fine, or a pleasant hello,
But the bubbling excitement of discovery and joy;
The wonder of life and love.

It is too hard!
Said I murmuring back
To the image in the mirror.
For there is never a day when things are just right,
Nor an hour of absolute peace.
Listen carefully and you'll understand,
Why this challenge, I cannot accept.

Nights are too short,
Morning hours so cold;
The buses, never on time.
The children so loud, and people so rude,
A slip on the ice, lost papers and tests.
A touch of the flu, and the all around blues,
Oh how can I conquer them all?

Now listen here
Boomed my conquering soul,
Your pains are all in your mind.
Life is a garden of roses and thorns,
The caretaker, none other than you.
Carefully pick, the rose from the thorns,
Be happy today,   I challenge you!

STAND FORTH ANE BE COUNTED

By Jean R. Moore

Do you recall the choosing of teams?
When there was some game to be played?
The captains would choose,
And we'd stand by their side
Until all were counted and tried.

The childhood games are over it seems,
But we still must be counted and tried.
And now is the time for us to decide
Which captain we'll follow in stride.

To speak and be heard, is a challenge indeed;
So much easier to rest in the shade.
But our Captain is calling, He needs us today
Sand forth and be counted, his law to obey.

CONSECRATE YOUR LIFE

THE STANDARDS WE LIVE

By Jean R. Moore 7-7-05

Regardless of our lot in life,
No matter where we stand;
Someone is watching
and learning from us;
appraising and judging
the Gospel plan.

It may be your smile,
or helping others in need;
or your example of love
that has planted a seed.

The Gospel to us
is something we give;
it is everyday life
and the standards we live.

FAITH

ADDED UPON

By Jean R. Moore

Added Upon in the glory of God
Sing praise and give thanks, His word is our rod.

My blessings again have been added upon in the temple of my
LORD.
My cup is full and over the brim; my thanks shall never grow dim.

My first temple trip as a youth was so sure…
doing baptisms for the dead. Then later my Endowment…
What a glorious privilege to be Added Upon, if I endure.

Each time that I went I was Added Upon with Knowledge, by spirit
and love.
Then came marriage and eternal covenants.
My heart swelled with faith and love.
But our union was barren and I longed for the gift,
The laughter and joy of children at home.

Each time that I went, the message the same…
Be patient. Have faith. Stay true.

Ten years and then one day a beautiful girl…again temple blessings…
Added Upon.
Five years more, of be patient, have faith.
Another day, a baby boy. Again…Added Upon
Another girl, another boy; another time to be Added Upon.

What a great blessing…the House of the LORD
To seal our family eternal and sure, A gift of the Gospel restored.

For we are again, Added Upon each time that we return.
Never ending the love in the truth that we learn
To have faith and be Added Upon.

Added Upon in the glory of God
Sing praise and give thanks his Word is our rod,
As we are eternally, Added Upon!

COUNCILS; A HEAVENLY PATTERN

By Jean Moore (3-3-97)

The council is a pattern divine,
Set forth by God, and called in His name.
For in the beginning, before our life here,
He called a council together,
    And as Family we came.

We reasoned and listened,
And discussed the great plan;
We voted and chose;
Then our journey began.

And here, as there, we must council together
In patience and love, and in harmony.
We should follow the pattern set forth above,
In the most basic of units, our family.

Council in faith,
Seek guidance in prayer,
And our Father in Heaven,
Will always be there!

CREATIONS OF GOD

By Jean R. Moore

The creations
Of God speak
The glory
Of His love;

As a tender rose
In June
I am one
Of these;

A creation
Of God.

GOD BLESS YOU PRECIOUS FRIEND

By Jean R. Moore

There speaks within my humble heart a special prayer for you.
A prayer to Him who reigns on high, who dwells amid the stars and sky.
Because this prayer was meant for you, a plea of love and care
I'll share dear friend, my thoughts with you, for they are righteous, good and true

I asked the Lord to be your guide,
To bless your mind with faith
To travel with you day and night
And keep your spirit burning bright.

I asked Him if He would walk with you
And clasp your humble hand,
To whisper strength and hope and truth
And help preserve your stainless youth.

But my dear friend you must recall
That these are only yours,
If you will call upon His name
And of His words, be not ashamed.

You must remember who you are
And who you said you would serve.
You must walk tall and straight and strong;
The path is long but must go on.

You see dear precious friend of mine, you are chosen of the Lord
To teach His Gospel plan of truth and magnify the call of youth.
The Lord will love and bless you there, if you but do His will.
For love and truth shall always be; the way to God's eternity.
And so these thoughts I leave with you, to ponder in your heart.
Upon your soul may they descend;
God Bless You Precious Friend!

MISSIONARY PRAYER

By Jean R. Moore (1975)

DEAR LORD;

You've asked of me a special thing
   A wondrous chance, you've given me;
   To preach and teach Thy holy word,
   Thy love and care: eternity.
From the very beginning when I lived with You;
   You taught me words that I should know;
   You prepared my lessons carefully
   and then You watched my spirit grow.
At last one day I came to earth, to a home of Gospel light,
   Where I was raised in righteousness
   As the child of an Israelite.
   Even as a reckless child, when life was fun and play,
My parents taught me Thy great plan
   And the joy of the Gospel way!
   I tried to follow every law that came from Thy great
   throne;
   I tried to live them every day from the example I'd
   been shown.
And now dear Lord as I depart, help me keep this Gospel truth,
   Help me spread Thy words of love, and stay a faithful
   youth.
   Help me live each passing day
   As though it were my last;
   Help me to show my friends dear Lord
   The beauty of our past.
Help them see the life before, and how it all began,
   Help them see the masterpiece of Thy eternal plan.
   Help me teach them all Thy words
   That I learned at home with Thee,
   Help them understand dear Lord
   That they shall live through eternity.

Help me to do all of these while I am teaching there,
Help me love the people Lord, and kneel with them
in prayer.
For this is one desire that's been with me since birth;
That I could preach Thy Gospel plan, to all the ends
of earth.
And now that dream of long ago, is waiting at the door,
I've got the key within my hand,
To blessings rich and sure.
AMEN.

PRAYER OF HOPE

By Jean R. Moore

The prayer of hope

Is folded

Softly

In the seeds

Of Faith.

THE BLESSING OF FAITH
...IS THE REWARD
OF DECISION.

...JEAN R. MOORE

TO EACH OF US

By Jean R. Moore

To each of us God gives a test
In different ways for different things
To try our faith, and test our love
To build our trust in Him above.

For only God can know my faith
And save my soul from sin,
The test I have, is mine alone,
and only I can win!

TRUST IN GOD

By Jean R. Moore

We must have trust in our God,
We must hold tightly to the iron rod.
We must keep faith for every day,
Don't think it's important to be so "mod".

God made man out of clay,
He wants our spirit to never stray.
Keep your faith, firm and strong,
Let it shine every day.

The road to heaven is straight and long,
Hold the iron with a cheerful song.
Strive to reach that heavenly throng,
And among God's chosen we'll belong.

FAMILIES

ETERNAL FAMILIES

By Jean R. Moore Oct. 2005

ALL
Children are part
Of
A family plan
A family dream,
A family work,
A family team.

For our Eternal Parent,
Father of us all
Has ordained this vast experience
In families large or small.

FAMILIES ARE ETERNAL

By Jean R. Moore 11-26-85

The family is eternal,
of this truth I'm sure;
But only if we heed the Word,
can this promise be secure.

For siblings tend to quarrel
Especially when they're young;
And early in the stage of life
The consequence…begun.

For if we are to merit
Eternal homes on high;
We must begin with love at home
And quarreling tongues must die.

Many are the friends we love
And think the bond is strong;
But when eternal ties are named,
To families we'll belong.

Yes, the family is eternal
Of this truth I'm sure;
But only if we heed the Word
Can His promise be secure.

FAMILY CIRCLE

By Jean R. Moore (10-13-87)

A family is a circle.

We all can belong.

In love and trust,

We build our home,

And make our circle strong

FIFTY YEARS IS NOT ENOUGH

By Jean Moore 10/4/10

Fifty years is not enough
To spend walking side by side,
Not enough to grow our love
Nor our feelings deep inside.

Fifty years is not enough
To gain patience here on earth
We must continue on and on
As our spirits learn rebirth.

Fifty years is not enough
Sharing life and love with you;
I'd like to share eternity
Making memories, pure and true.

ORDAINED OF GOD

By Jean Moore 2-1-2016

Apostles and prophets have told us again,
that marriage is sacred, for the children of men.
It cannot be changed by fashion or whim,
nor broken or mocked, without offending HIM.

The marriage bond between a woman and man,
is ordained of God and part of His plan.
Mortal laws cannot alter, change or unmake,
the divine order of GOD, nor His laws forsake.

Let us be faithful, obedient and true,
For marriage is sacred and eternal too!

MISSIONARY BROTHER

By Jean R. Moore (June 1963)

I know I'm just a little girl,
With not too much to say
Anything very important that is,
On such an important day.

Yet, I'm as proud as punch today,
To see my brother go
On a mission for our wonderful church,
Although I'll miss him so.

He may not miss me much, I'm 'fraid,
I've teased and pestered lots,
But I do love him, loads and loads,
And so express my careful thoughts.

If he will work with all his might
While he is overseas,
I'll try my best while I'm at home,
To make him proud of me.

He'll be remembered in all my prayers,
And also in between,
Before I know it, he'll be back
To see his little Jean.

PRECEPTS EVERLASTING

By Jean R. Moore 1/26/86

The teaching of our childhood
Persist throughout the years
And often, how we meet the test,
Or how we feel inside…
Or why we do the things we do;
We learned at mother's side.

Let each home be one of prayer…
Of learning, faith and fasting;
And may each child in later years,
Remember wisdom taught at home;
and of precepts everlasting.

STRENGTHENING OUR FAMILIES

By Jean R. Moore (8-5-01)

Take the time
To strengthen the home,
As the prophets have counseled,
In family groups or alone.

Learn from the scriptures,
Sing songs of praise,
Be joyful together,
And obedient all your days.

It will foster love,
Invite the spirit,
Strengthen solidarity,
And inspire deeds of merit.

THE RISING GENERATION

By Jean R. Moore 9/17/10

The promise of the future
Is in the teachings of the past,
We must teach the rising generation,
Values, that will last.

It is our divine responsibility,
To nurture, teach, and guide
This rising generation,
Of the path they must decide.

Motherhood and Fatherhood
Are eternal in their reach,
And we must live this principle
In the Gospel that we teach.

GOALS

A PETITION

By Jean R. Moore 8-72

Dear FATHER up in heaven, so loving and so wise,
I come before Thee on bended knee, and with a humble heart.
To set before Thee a petition which speaks my restless part.
My Lord, My God, while I am yet so young;
while I am yet so full of grace,
Call me to share from place to place.
With my voice I cry unto Thee, for in my heart is whispered hope,
As I kneel before Thee Lord, my desire is very simple.
I will ask neither glory nor wide acclaim,
But just the call of serving;
To be chosen by Thy wisdom to work in serving Thee.

Everything, which I possess, belongs to Thee alone,
Every blessing that is mine came from Thy great throne.
I want to labor in Thy vineyard, until Thy children have been told
Of Thy great and glorious name.
And called them to Thy fold.

But FATHER, in the sky,
You are much more wise than I
and I will not ask this blessing now
If it is not Thy mind and will.

AN EQUALIZING GIFT

By Jean R. Moore 1985

There is an equalizing gift,

Awarded to us all.

No exceptions to the rule,
Nor concessions great or small.
It is the same for bond or free,
For ignorant or wise,
For those with faith, and those without,
There is no compromise.
This quality is friend or foe,
Our master or our prime,
And we must conquer if we can:
The gift that we call TIME.

BE CREATIVE AND FRUGAL

By Jean Moore (Feb. 2001)

In today's world of shiny and new
We have forgotten
How to make do.

We have learned how to want,
much more than we need,
and learned how to get it
then say it's
not greed.

The stores are so close and their wares are so fine;
It's so easy to shop, just going on line.

Buy new and spend more is the trend we have set,
It's so easy to charge it, and soon we're in debt.

Maybe it's time to remember the past,
Take stock of the world
and make things to last.

Fix up what we have, and wear what we've got
Be creative and frugal
and content to "have not."

FIX IT UP, WEAR IT OUT
MAKE IT DO OR DO WITHOUT

BUY THE TEMPORAL LAMP FIRST

By Jean Moore Oct. 2007

No one may know, the day nor the hour,
When the LORD in His glory
Will come in great power.
But we are commanded to watch and prepare,
To study the signs,
With discernment and prayer.

While filling our lamp
With spiritual oil
Let us not forget
To buy the lamp
In the first place!

CLIMB HIGH

By Jean Moore (1970?)

Climb the tallest mountain,
Spill over every crest.
Keep reaching for an eagle's crown,
Until you've proved the test.

So reach into the highest stars
And capture every dream
The powers of earth can't hold you down.
How hard though it may seem.

The eagle is king of all the sky,
His boundaries are untouched.
His wings will never cease to fly
Into the endless sky.

So reach into the highest stars
And capture every dream.
The powers of earth can't hold you down
How hard, though they may seem.

…the powers of earth, can't hold you down
How hard though they may seem.

DESIRE IS THE KEY

By Jean R. Moore

What are your plans?
What are your goals?
Do you expect to attain them
Through treacherous shoals?

There's just one small item
That you can't do without,
And that is: Desire,
to be without doubt

When the going gets tough
and your goal seems lost;
Remember the key;
That your plan has a cost.

There's nothing for FREE
In this world of ours
Not even your life
Or the light spring showers.

So remember this key
for use every day.
You'll aspire to the top,
'cause there's no other way!

DON'T LET HIM DOWN

By Jean R. Moore

If in the course of earthly life,
We find our soul in toil and strife;
Remember Christ, His life and light,
Defend your goals, keep them in sight.

You've set your goals, keep them high
Keep them aspiring to the endless sky;
Keep your soul spotless and clean,
Defend your virtue and self-esteem.

Life is a gift, directed by God,
Created and made by His own hand.
Don't let Him down, or what He has planned,
Don't be moved like the shifting sand.

GOALS FOREVER

By Jean Moore

The goals you don't set today or tomorrow,
May lead you to your future sorrow.

You must start right today,
Or tomorrow's events will bring what they may.

If you don't set them for your life;
You will forever be in conflict and strife.

The goals you make within your heart,
You must do all and not just part.

Don't let them sit there waiting for you,
You have to try and work a little too!

You must make your aims today,
To reap tomorrow's golden pay.

So let your goals be high and tall,
And keep them rolling like a giant ball.

When you have proven worthy someday,
God, to all His faithful will say:

You have proven a loyal soul,
Now wear this crown of eternal goals.

Keep it, love it, and treasure it high,
For now and forever, you will never die!

GOALS OF YOUTH

By Jean R. Moore

The goals of youth
Are the tools
Of eternity.
Secured snugly
In the
Seeds
Of FAITH!
Use them well…

JUST YESTERDAY
By Jean R. Moore

Just yesterday it seemed to me that I was just a child;
Just yesterday, I started school,
And I was young and wild!
I remember when I wrote my name, and then my mommy's too,
I still can see her glossy smile
When I scribbled "I LOVE YOU"

I remember then how proud I was to carry home a book,
And how I worked so long and hard
To read this tale I took.
For just a day or two ago, my friends were very near;
Everything was fine and sure,
And all my plans were clear.
But when I looked into the skies, and saw the countless stars;
I thought how tiny I must be
Compared to God's eternity.

I still can see the cherry trees that bloomed in early spring,
And I can smell the flavored air
Those blossoms used to bring.
As the years went fleeting by; my mind grew strong and wise;
And I began to realize
How quickly our time flies!
Just yesterday, it seemed to me that I was young and gay;
Life was long and beautiful
And games were meant to play.
Now my school years are done and legally I'm free,
And memories flood my weary heart
Of things I used to be.

I remember things I learned, and the precious friends I knew.
I'll not forget, I'll not forsake; to these memories I'll be true.
And as the years go fleeting by; my mind grows strong and wise,
And I can slowly realize how quickly our time flies!

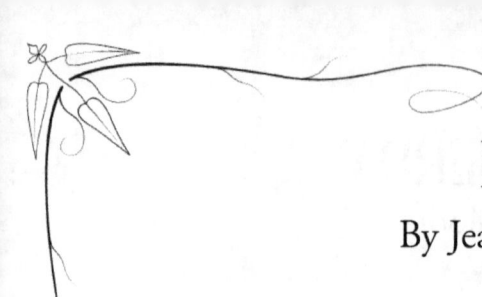

LIFE
By Jean R. Moore

Life….

A reflection of the past

And

A promise of the future.

Happy birthday!

Make everyday count
For something!

OF ONE HEART AND MIND

By Jean Moore 9-07

Be of one heart,
Of one mind,
Of one cause.
Be true to yourself,
To our God,
And His laws.

A house cannot stand
Divided and broken,
It must be united,
As prophets have spoken.

Begin with yourself in all that you do,
"This above all…to thine own self be true."
(Shakespeare)
At one in your thoughts,
In your words, in your deeds;
At one with your God;
He will succor your needs!
Unity is—the great hallmark of truth,
The standard of victory
The power of youth.
Be of one heart,
Of one mind,
Of one cause;
Be faithful and sure,
To our God,
And his laws.

SEARCH AND GAIN WISDOM

By Jean R. Moore

TIME: is a concept of life,

LIFE; an experience of learning

LEARNING; the objects of progress…

Therefore;

SEARCH…. and gain wisdom to your soul

Until your joy in life is full.

SO TEMPORARY

By Jean R. Moore

Youth …ah so temporary, so perfect
So innocent yet so full of guilt,
For that is the time,
When dreams are built,

The time in life when spring is fresh,
The time in life when love is clean,
The time in life when love's a dream.

The time in life when play is fun,
The time in life when you are young.
The time in life when grass is green
And all the world is soft and clean.

Now is the time to build this dream,
Now is the time to make it gleam;
Now is the time for you to learn;
To make it grow and make it true,
To make it "live' is up to you!

GOSPEL

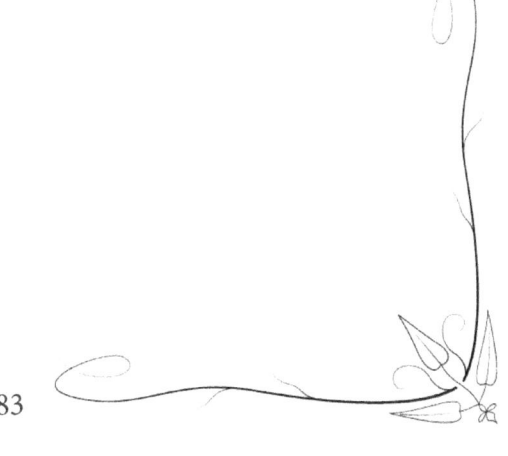

ABIDE IN HOPE AND PRAYER

By Jean Moore 10-86

Every amber ray of dawn;
Every blossom in the spring;
Every rainbow in the clouds,
Evokes a hope of future things.

And when in times of sorrow,
or in shadows of despair;
Recall the promise, and the blessing:
And abide in hope and prayer.

THE BOOK OF MORMON: BEACON FOR OUR DAY

By Jean Moore 9/6/05

A beacon for our day
The Book of Mormon shows the way.
It is our guide in times of trial
And our staff for an extra mile;
It is our comfort in the day of sorrow
And our compass to chart the 'morrow
It is our strength when we are downed
And our joy when we are found;
It is the keystone of faith,
The scepter of truth;
The doctrine of life,
And the map for our youth.

CONSIDER YOUR DEBT

By Jean Moore (7-86)

There is a debt you owe the LORD
A tenth of all your gain
But wonder aloud
Have you discharged?
Fair share of your domain?

Consider the talents
He gave to you;
Your joy, your love, your song;
Consider your time,
Your health, your work…

And most of all;

Consider His gift to man;
Your knowledge of truth,
And His plan.

Consider the debt you owe the LORD;
A tenth of all your gain;

Consider aloud
Have you discharged?
Fair share of your domain?

EMPIRE STONE ROLLING FORTH

By Jean Moore V.T. message 11-05

The stone has been cut....
Not with hands, nor man-made.
It will continue to grow....
And its Realm never fade.

For this is the Kingdom
Of CHRIST our LORD;
This conquest by love
And not of the sword.

As envisioned by Daniel
And prophets of old
This kingdom by faith
Was foreseen and foretold.

It will fill every heart
Every sorrow amend.
It will fill the whole earth
Its domain never ends.

ETERNAL VOW

By Jean R. Moore

An eternal vow, is that of marriage,
We will ride forever,
In this beautiful carriage.

Marriage is sacred for young and for old,
We must be wise,
If her treasures we'll hold.

The one who you choose to be stainless and clean,
The one you adore,
Should eternally beam.

We will glide upon wings soaring above,
We will cherish and keep
This carriage of love.

We need to remember, it is not just for earth,
It carries within it
Eternal rebirth.

Eternal the vow and high is the crown,
Everlasting the choice
Of the one you have found.

Let your devotion be lasting and long,
And timeless the beauty
In your gentle song.

To make this vow sacred should be your endeavor,
Remember one thing…
Love is forever!

GREATER LOVE

By Jean R. Moore

A friend is great in the eyes of God,
For greater love hath no man,
than to lay down his life
for that of another,
And to respectfully love
The life of a brother.

To be a friend, and have a friend,
Is greater far than treasured gold,
It is reaching for the highest stars,
and finding God within their bars.

To you my friend I give great thanks,
for being you, and being true;
for being great, in a special way,
for being kind, each lasting day.

Now I'll say, just one good-by
For memories last all through the years.
They will last through time, life and tears.
They will keep us clean and free from fears.

So think of God while you are away,
Remember truth and you will not stray.
REMEMBER love,
REMEMBER faith
REMEMBER GOD,
And how to pray.

HIS HOLY HOUSE

By Jean R. Moore (Provo Temple)

The Spires
Of His Holy House
Will Sparkle in the sun.

And I was there
For thought and prayer
When His temple
Was begun!!

IS THERE A PLACE?

By Jean R. Moore

Is there a place of peace and prayer?
Is there a haven from hate and despair?
Is there a shield from fear and sin?
Is there a shelter that is safe within?

Is there a place?
…where the heart may rest,
…the spirit quest,
…the mind grow strong,
…and the soul finds song?

Is there a Home of Glory and Love?
…of learning and order, as in heaven above?
Is there a Home, so divine?

As God has counseled…
It could be mine!

ISRAEL

By Jean Moore

ISRAEL.....

Is not a place to see,
But an experience to feel;

Not a history to retrace,
But a memory to uncase;

Not a religion to inspect,
But understanding and respect;

Not a people to observe,
But an inheritance to preserve;

Not a culture to learn,
But a lineage to discern;

Not a dogma of devotion,
But a fountain of emotion;

Not a chronicle of the Bible sum
But of prophecy yet to come;

Not a land in which to wander,
But an experience in which to ponder.

Israel.

LORD'S TIME

By Jean R. Moore
(1987)

Forgive me if I hurry on,
And cannot long postpone…
For I am on an errand now,
And this time is not my own.

I must be about His work
Without delay or whim
For the errand is the Lord's you see,
And this time belongs to Him.

MY DIVINE NATURE

By Jean Moore
4-2006 (VT Message)

The vale was drawn,
our memories gone;
but my divine nature
glows on
like the dawn.
For I am a daughter
of infinite worth,
From the mansions of glory
I have come down to earth.

We must train up our minds
and busy our hands;
make ready our spirits,
in working God's plans.
For our divine nature
is of loving
and learning;
of serving
and giving,
and gracefulness yearning.
For unto our FATHER,
We will be returning.

MY GARDEN

By Jean R. Moore

Droplets of silver, edge the green;
Whispers of grass, hang low with ease.
The feathers of life are in the scene,
And the Angel of love descends from on high.

I say in my heart, what a peaceful place,
What a lovely way to feel His grace.
Then I see light in the glory of God,
How great the splendor, this diving sight.

He speaks to me; we walk along,
And in my heart, there grows a song.
Deep in the trees of violet shadow,
The leaves dance lightly on the soft spring breeze.

Morning descends in the glory of spring,
I vision the past and see my King.
The hour was gone, too soon it seemed;
Of the angel of light, that came to redeem.

NO MORE STRANGERS

By Jean R. Moore
(music also written by Jean)

In the final judgement call
When the Lord rules over all
There will be among His numbered sheep
Those adopted great and small.
It will make no difference then
What our heritage began;
But rather if we kept His law
And lived the Master's Plan.

Ye are no longer foreigners
But fellow citizens.
Adopted in the covenant
And of the household of God.

In a world of many creeds
And of people...bond and free
There might be times I feel better than
A brother in his need.
But the family will extend
And the blessings gather in
All races, tongues, and nations...
Adopted as His seed.

Ye are no longer foreigners
But fellow citizens.
Adopted in the covenant
And of the household of God.

PRIESTHOOD...
A GIFT TO ALL

By Jean R. Moore 1/94

The Priesthood is authority
Given from God to man;
To guide our paths and bless our lives,
As part of His great plan.

This blessing God imparts to all
Who are worthy of His name;
To bond and free, to young and old,
To rich or poor…we're all the same.

To comfort in a time of need,
To bless when sick or ill;
To strengthen when alone or scared,
To re-assure, inspire and fill.

To each of us is given this gift
To search and strongly seek,
But wisdom is pre-requisite…
Your soul submissive, humble, meek.

The priesthood is the power of God
Released to men on earth;
To use in righteousness and love,
To bless our lives from birth.

SONNET 2/73

(Masterpiece of God)
By Jean R. Moore

Beginning with the birth of breath and bloom,
The grandeur of God's glory, full is here,
And all the earth is balmy with perfume,
That sweetens with each season of the year;
And though I've never seen him face to face,
But ever have I heard His soothing voice,
I'm sure I've seen the beauty of His grace,
And heard the songs of angels in rejoice;
I've walked the path where He may once have trod,
And peered into the spacious skies above,
For all the world's the masterpiece of God,
And all bare witness of His gentle love;
The evidence is here for all to see
God lives and speaks the same as you and me.

STEEPLES OF GLORY

By Jean R. Moore

The steeples of God's glory
Emitted the magnitude
Of His majesty;
And the children of His creation
Sealed their love
Together
With the solemn
Vow of eternity
Upon their lips

THE SWEET GIFT OF PROPHECY

By Jean R. Moore 9-97

We live in an age when things are uncertain;
The future…opaque as the folds of a curtain.
But the Lord has not left us afraid or alone;
He has blessed us with prophets
And our future foreshown.

Into each life, when righteously sought,
…the sweet gift of prophecy is spiritually taught.
Be not discouraged, in doubt or in fear,
Press forward with faith, great hope,
And good cheer.

THE GIFT

By Jean R. Moore
V.T. 3-94

The Savior promised when He left this earth,
A comforter to guide and lift;
To teach us and to whisper truth
The Holy Ghost is such a gift.

I pondered deeply which choice was right,
Which way would bring the greatest light.
Then choosing what I though was best,
My heart swelled warm with sweet delight.

I mourned the loss of my dear friend,
And cried for comfort; my darkest hour.
Again it came, soothing heart and soul,
The peace and strength of a Higher Power.

I studied with profound intent…
A hundred times in strained review,
Until at length upon my knees,
My mind was cleared, I though anew.

I queried in my heart and mind;
What is the truth? How shall I know?
Then listening with humble trust…
The answer came, sweet, soft, and slow.

The Savior promised as He left this earth,
A Comforter to guide, and lift.
To teach us and to whisper truth…
How blessed are we with such a Gift!

TO BE WITHOUT GUILE

By Jean Moore 4/15/15

What does it mean to be without guile?
To be without ruse, deception, or lies.
It would mean to be holy, childlike, and pure,
To be more like our Savior, humble and wise.

In this world of sin, growing darkness and pain,
To be without guile is our highest aim.
To be honest and true and keep our heart pure,
Is more urgent now, than ever before.

WHAT OF THE GODHEAD

By Jean Moore 1/05

The nature of the Godhead for centuries past

has been a question many scholars have asked.

The truth had been lost but now is restored:

Knowledge and power and priesthood assured.

A glorified Man is our Father divine,

His Son Jesus Christ, your brother and mine.

Each one distinct yet united in plan

Their purpose is one, the salvation of man.

A personage of spirit, the Holy Ghost brings

a witness to us: the truth of all things.

With understanding comes love and the will to obey;

to follow His plan and walk in His way.

WHEN I AM HUMBLE

By Jean Moore Oct. 5, 04

When I am humble I look to the Lord
I feel of His Love,
And gain His reward.

I listen to counsel
And follow His will
I am respectful and reverent
Submissive, and still.

I am more willing to listen
More anxious to hear,
More tender of feeling,
And absent of fear.

"Be thou humble and the Lord thy God
shall lead thee by the hand..." (D.&C. 112:10)
and give thee direction
for every command.

WORTH THE GAIN

By Jean R. Moore

Whatever the cost, whatever the pain,
Whatever the struggle; It's worth the gain.

But what could be so valuable?
And what could be so sure?
What is the gift, prized more than life?
That's worth so much to endure?

Not always prompt in blessings, not earthly in reward;
Not always clearly evident, it is the promise of the Lord.

For eyes have never seen, and ears have never heard,
Nor entered in the heart of man…the promise of His Word.

Whatever the cost, whatever the pain,
Whatever the struggle; it's worth the gain!!

GRATITUDE

A SACRED GIFT

By Jean Moore

The Lord, A sacred gift has given me,

And I must keep it holy

Then the promise of His love,

Will follow me forever.

BEFORE THE WORLD WAS... REMEMBER?

By Jean Moore 1970 ?

Dear God;
I used to live with you, away up in the sky,
I used to walk and talk with you, alone, just you and I.

Remember when you'd walk with me,
in the forest of silver dew?
Remember how the trees grew tall,
in the lightened sky of blue?
We walked around the shining lakes,
and watched the drifting swan.
We saw the clearness of the sky
in the purple rays of dawn.

We walked among the rolling hills,
and saw the golden grain.
We saw the drifting clouds float by,
and felt the cleansing rain.
We saw the deer glide gracefully
in pines of green and gold;
We watched the night fall softly
and all your throne enfold.

We walked around the garden there,
and viewed the gift of love,
We touched the faith of love itself...
descending like a dove.
Remember when you'd talk to me,
and tell me all your plans?
Remember all the things you said,
about this wonderland?

You said it would be very hard,
and really test my trust;
You said there'd be a devil here,
who'd tempt me with fear and lust.
You told me all that I should do,
to stay on solid ground.
You said that there'd be prophets here,
to keep me homeward bound.

You told me to be very strong,
in things I knew were right,
You said you'd help me out a bit,
by giving Gospel light.
You said you'd give me lots of friends,
and gifts that I could share,
You said you'd give me lots of love
for all the people there.

Remember when I lived with you, away up in the sky?
I used to walk and talk with you, alone, just you and I.

GRATITUDE

By Jean R. Moore

What debt of gratitude is mine,
To Him who reigns on high;
What words of thankfulness I give,
To the God up in the sky!

I dwelt with Him away up there,
With God, the human maker.
My spirit there was pure and clean,
For He had been my shaper.

Everyday He blesses me
With love and life and breath,
And everyday I'll live my best
Until my soul meets death.

And now within this earthly state,
I'll speak with Him in prayer
Until again I live with Him
In the heavens way up there!

HAPPINESS

By Jean R. Moore

Happiness is like
A rolling wheel:

The more we have,
The more we give,
The more we share,
The more we feel…

Happiness is like
A boomerang:

We need to throw
It away
Before
It can return…

Happiness begets love,
Love begets service,
Service begets happiness,
And the circle
Is complete.

Happiness
Is an attitude,

And we are master
Of our joy!

MORE GRATITUDE GIVE ME

By Jean R. Moore
(July 1995)

The purr of a cat so soothing and soft;
Fresh sparkles of rain,
Refreshing and clear,
This land of the patriots,
So mighty and free,
My children, my home, so simple, so dear.

Unto God I give thanks,
For these gifts are all from Him.
Unto God I sing great Praise,
With all of my soul,
Through all of my days.

RAINBOWS IN THE RAIN
By Jean R. Moore

I walked along in hues of rain and watched the rolling clouds.
I thought of all the people, drifting, like the clouds.

For all the people here you know are just like drops of rain.
They fall upon the puddle world and here they all remain.

They never really leave; they never really stay,
They only leave their memories, which linger day to day.

They are all a different color like rainbows way up high,
Like every different raindrop that oozes from the sky.

And in between the mountains, the rainbows spread their gold;
For me and you and everyone, their treasures they unfold.

And like the rainbows in the sky, the people share their skill.
For me and you and everyone, our hearts they try to fill.

THANKFUL HEART

By Jean Moore

A thankful heart

Is the reward

Of God's gift

To man…

LOVE

THE DEBT

By Jean R. Moore (2/10/1986)

You have said I give too much,
And you have nothing to return;
So I shall ask but one request,
To ease your deep concern.

The task is easy you will say, and seems as naught at all;
But there will be a time to come when the mountain will stand tall.

It is now my time to love, my time to share and give;
For I have both the time and means and nothing to renege.
But there will be a time for you,
To give your time away;
To give your life as I have done,
Then the debt you shall repay.

To share with one who needs your help;
 and live your life so pure…
That others will in time be led, to that great eternal door.

That's all I ask…a simple task,
Yet difficult at times;
But you will find your life entwined
With love and light divine.
It's not to me you owe a debt, nor to the world abroad,
But fill your heart with pure intent…
AND RENDER IT TO GOD!

JESUS CHRIST

BRIDGES

By Jean R. Moore
6/15/13

What kind of bridge
are you crossing today?
Is it safe and secure,
as you pass on your way?

Have you built up your life
with study and care?
Have you strengthened the pillars
with Faith, Hope, and Prayer?

For there layeth in wait
the Destroyer of all
His goal is deception,
to make your Bridge fall.

The Master Builder is calling
each individual one,
To cross on HIS bridge
through Jesus Christ His Son.

His pathway is narrow,
but His bridge is secure,
He is calling to you,
and He waits at the door!

BE MINE

By Jean Moore 2-24

Be Mine, says He,
To both young and old.
My love is sufficient,
Gather in to My fold.

Give Me your heart,
Your might, mind and soul,
And I will return
Your measure in full.

Be Mine, says He;
I have paid the whole price,
Give Me your devotion,
I AM;
JESUS CHRIST

EASTER MORN, WHAT A GLORIOUS DAY

By Jean Moore 4-1-21

They witness the entry, and the waving of palms,
Foretold by prophets,
In Glory and psalms.
Heartache for us in the Garden of Tears,
Bowed 'neath the load of our sin and fears.

The trial and mocking, the scourging and grief,
Then nailed to a cross, like an ordinary thief.
The anointing with oils, hearts heavy with gloom,
The Passover Lamb, in a borrowed tomb.

Then came the dawn and in splendor we sing,
The Risen LORD, as Master and King!
Easter morn, what a glorious day,
All blessings are ours, if we only obey.

IN THE IMAGE OF GOD

By Jean Moore 3-3-16

We are created in the image of God,
With eyes and ears, and heart and mind;
To love, and work, and help one another,
To develop our gifts and our talents in kind.

How silly to think of GOD without form;
As some kind of thought, or undefined blob.
He says what He means, and means what He said,
All men were created in the image of GOD.

In this troubled world, we often can't see,
How divine is our image, how like GOD we can be.

GOD gave us ears to hear: voice,
Just like Him.
He gave us eyes to see: love,
Just like Him.
He gave us a mouth to speak: prayer,
Just like Him.
A heart to feel compassion,
Just like Him.
We are in image…
JUST LIKE HIM!

IN TUNE

By Jean Moore (10-82)

How shall you recognize His voice?
If you have never listened
To the whisperings of His Spirit?

How shall you recognize His Handiwork?
If you have never
Pondered His power?

How shall you find His Path?
If you have never walked
In His footsteps?

How shall you know of His Law?
If you have never lived
His commandments?

How shall you be His Disciple?
If you have never been
His friend?

JUST BY CHANCE?

By Jean R. Moore

I saw the sky laced with pillowy clouds,
I watched them sway, frolic and dance;
And I asked in my heart, why is there question,
How could this have happened, Just by Chance?

I looked at the pumpkins, the squash, and the corn;
I noticed their pattern, their color and form.
Not one is the same, no two are alike,
But all have a pattern, that's followed quite tight.

Life is a gift, directed by God,
Created and made by His great hand;
The living, the dead, the sea and the land,
Bear witness to me, that there is a God!

Others may laugh and think it not so,
The world just happened, as the talk may go.
But I know for myself, that just isn't true;
I know there's a God, who made me and you!

LET US SEEK LIGHT

By Jean R. Moore

Light is the essence of Glory
And Glory, the nature of God;
For God is the Light, and Life of the world,
His Light shows the path we would trod.

There is no glory in darkness
For Satan is ruler of sin.
There is no sharing or giving
Only taking, and keeping within.

So let us seek light and reflection
Be wise in the path that we trod.
For Light is the essence of Glory,
And Glory; the nature of God!

NOT MERELY A MAN

By Jean R. Moore 12/1996 (Germany)

An acquaintance of mine, now many years past,
Laughed at my faith, and scoffing...he asked.
How can you believe in these fairy-tale stories?
Of this man called Jesus, and his made up glories.
Why, no man can turn the water to wine
Nor open the light to eyes that are blind.

No man can heal with only a word;
These things are impossible and clearly absurd
No man can command the wind and the waves,
Nor unstop the door, to those sleeping in graves.
No man can restore what clearly is lost,
You worship a myth, you have been double-crossed!

I said, you're right to his utter surprise
No man can perform as the Bible testifies.

But this Jesus Christ was not merely a man;
Not merely a myth, and not earthly in plan.
He is the CHRIST, the King of all Kings;
He is the Messiah, and Lord of all things.
He is the Creator, and God of this earth
No wonder the angels sang at His birth.
No wonder the heavens were ablaze with starlight
And the shepherds and wise came seeking this sight.
He is not merely a man, but of lineage divine;
Not merely a man, BUT YOUR GOD AND
MINE!

ONE OF THE LEAST OF THESE

BY Jean Moore 5-24-17

I am one of the least of these;
Not great in power or wisdom or might.
But by serving me,
Ye are serving **HIM;**
gaining in wisdom and greater light.
"Ye have done it unto me."
Matt. 25:40

OUR FAITH IN CHRIST WILL SEE US THROUGH

By Jean R. Moore (Apr. 2001)

When temptations are high and our troubles are too...
Our Faith in Christ
Will see us through.

When disappointment is strong, and successes are few...
Our Faith in Christ
Will see us through.

When death separates us from love that is true,
Our Faith in Christ
Will see us through.

When our struggles are many, and our outlook is blue...
Our Faith in Christ
Will see us through!

SON RISE

By Jean R. Moore (4-19-73)

Sunrise,

For the birth of men.

SONRISE

From the gift of God.

The promise of life

Is open to all;

The glory of God.
To both great and small.

The Shepherd of men.
In glory and love;

Has risen this day
To His mansions above.

SON RISE,

For the pure in heart.

SON RISE,

The Eternal door!

SONNET 4-73

Crown of Glory
By Jean R. Moore

The power to teach, is the power to guide
And the power to guide is the glory of love;
The gift of love is something felt inside
Which teaches truth and cometh from above.
A teacher finds the gold that's hidden in
The mind; and then he teaches how to mold,
And shape, and fit, the precious truth within
The heart of youth, that's waiting to unfold.
A teacher walked the shores of Galilee
And taught the people there to love and share;
He taught the glory of eternity
And filled the world with beauty everywhere.
The greatest teacher man has ever known
Has walked the path to greatness all alone.

(Now wears the crown of glory on His throne.)

SUPPER OF REMEMBRANCE

By Jean R. Moore

The Lord has invited you

To the supper of His remembrance.

….Have you enough love to:

Prepare your heart,

Cleanse your mind,

Refresh your soul…

AND WORSHIP HIM?

LOVE

ETERNAL VOW

By Jean R. Moore

An eternal vow, is that of marriage,
We will ride forever,
In this beautiful carriage.

Marriage is sacred for young and for old,
We must be wise,
If her treasures we'll hold.

The one who you choose to be stainless and clean,
The one you adore,
Should eternally beam.

We will glide upon wings soaring above,
We will cherish and keep
This carriage of love.

We need to remember, it is not just for earth,
It carries within it
Eternal rebirth.

Eternal the vow and high is the crown,
Everlasting the choice
Of the one you have found.

Let your devotion be lasting and long,
And timeless the beauty
In your gentle song.

To make this vow sacred should be your endeavor,
Remember one thing...
Love is forever!

FRIENDSHIP IS A CIRCLE

By Jean Moore

Friendship is a circle

Growing like a seed.

The only way

to have a friend

Is be a friend

In deed!

IN ALL THINGS, IT IS SHOWN

By Jean R. Moore 1/04

As I ponder life's gifts and trials
from which I have grown;
I am reminded…God loves me,
and in all things… it is shown.

As I bathe or do the dishes
in the water clean and pure,
I know the LORD surely loves me,
of this truth, I am sure!

As I eat fruits of the garden
and there observe the ordered beauty,
I am reminded the LORD loves me,
and gratitude is my duty.

As I read from the scriptures,
so simple and so true;
I know again that the LORD loves me,
and this I know…I love Him too!

LANGUAGE OF THE SOUL

By Jean R. Moore 1-1-86

Silent thoughts and ponderings;
The language of the soul
is felt within the human heart
and makes the blessings full.

The brilliant hues of sunset,
or thoughts before a prayer;
a child with the gift of life,
or nature everywhere…

Have you listened to your thoughts?
have you pondered life and death?
Have you waited for the answers
in the Lord's eternal breath?

Has there been time….
in your schedules and mission,
To meditate;
Be still
And listen?

LOVE MY SON

By Jean Moore
(for Karen D)

TEACH   my son, give him education;
Teach him in the ways of God,
And in the ways of man.

SHOW   my son, give him destination,
Show him to be wise and strong,
And fill his heart with song.

HEAR   my son, give him comprehension;
Listen to his words of trial,
And help him understand.

KNOW   my son, give him inspiration,
Understand his heavy load
And help him find the road.

LOVE   my son, give him exaltation,
Love him with the kindest heart,
And with the richest part.

LOVE

By Jean R. Moore

Love is the gift
Of special care,
Love is my friend,
Who is always there.
Love is the word
Which means "I'll share".
Love is the Lord
Who hears my prayer.

Love is the voice
That sooths my fear,
Love is the thought
Which dries a tear;
Love is the heart
Who waits to hear,
Love is the soul
Who spreads good cheer.
Love is the eternal bond
Between your SAVIOR and you.

THOSE WHO HAVE LEARNED

By Jean R. Moore

Life is a concert of many tunes
Both harsh and soothing employ.

But those who have learned
to love one another
Feel the warmth of compassion
and the comfort of Joy.

TIMELESS MAGIC

By Jean R. Moore

As we love one another
We are more desirous to serve;
As we give ourselves in service
Our countenance is brimmed with happiness.
As our happiness spreads and deepens
so our heart is filled
with sweet and abiding love.

And the timeless magic of happiness
Circles and spreads,
Refreshed and re-fed;
Circles and spreads,
Refreshed and re-fed.

TOLD AND RETOLD

By Jean R. Moore

The shadows of hope
are flickering low.
The fire of life,
only a glow.
But the whisper
of faith
speaks
silver and gold;
And the story of love…
told and

retold!

NATURE

CHARIOT WINGS

By Jean R. Moore

The wind is always by my side.
It floats along in a graceful stride.
I love to see her dance and play
With the weeds on a summer's day.

Upon her wings, I would like to fly
But it is a dream, and I'll just sigh.
The wind can sometimes be my friend,
Her mysteries make me just pretend.

She sweeps the popcorn clouds along,
And in my ear, blows a song.
She feels so good on a sizzling day,
I love to see her rock and sway.

She raps and taps on my back door,
And creeps along the quiet floor.
She blows the stars on a windswept night,
Behind the clouds and out of sight.

The wind can dance in the village court,
And makes it seem like wonderful sport.
When we have the county fair,
She always has to be right there!

On my head she beats her breast;
It seems as though she will never rest.
Through the leaves she whistles and sings,
Carrying seeds on her chariot wings.

COTTON IN THE SKY

By Jean R. Moore

Cotton is the thing of which clouds are made
and cotton in the sky will never quite fade.

She drapes her wings over green and grassy hills,
the hungry creek beds, she almost fills.

In the soft light of early morning dawn,
she is found hiding a newborn fawn.

The sun tries to see through her think walls of cotton,
but the rays are hidden and almost forgotten.

The bright morning sun streaks through her winds,
and the animal kingdom awakens and sings.

Clouds in the sky can form a wall
and the way to heaven becomes just a hall.

She settles down to choke a tree
but the wings of a bird will ever fly free.

She hides the stars on a cotton night,
behind her wings and out of sight.

On smoldering days, I would like to ride,
upon her wings that skip and glide.

She hides the mountains from my sight
the deep snowy peaks she will ride all night.

I would like to fly on the wings of a cloud,
but with this gift, I am not endowed.

The pearled clouds will never sleep
she will keep her cotton soft and deep.

A stair to heaven she will provide,
but the way, she will always hide.

FROZEN CRYSTALS

By Jean R. Moore

I see the snow in the early morn,
the radiant world she will adorn.
The snow is diamonds in the air;
she bares no worry and has no care.

She is found wherever I go,
on every peak,
there is drifted snow.
The snow will fall on lakes of glass;
the water here will never pass.

The snow can hide the starry night,
behind her clouds and out of sight.
She can wrap the barren trees,
with crystal snow and silver leaves.

The snow can hide the frozen ground,
and place on it a crystal crown.
The snow will fall from far above,
and fill the earth with Heaven's love.

GOLDEN SPLENDOR

By Jean R. Moore

The sun is melting in the sky,
the clouds are pink
with sunset's glow.
The world is darkened
by the shadow
as the sun
is dropping low.

Crimson pink and velvet red
fills the sky in evening light.
In this beauty, I bow my head,
as the sun sinks out of sight.

The sun is now behind the peaks,
stars in heaven begin to shine.
The beauty there, all artists seek,
but the sun is now behind the line.

I LOVE THE RAIN

By Jean R. Moore

I love the rain, light and clear,
it ripples in the water mirror.
The rain can made me feel glad,
her purity, I wish I had.
The rain can speak to me all day,
wherever I go on my way.
I love the smell the rain will bring,
the laughing streams, she will make to sing.
I love the soft rain on my face; she makes me hum to her pace.
She leaves the world wet and still, and lakes and ponds, she will fill.

I WOULD LIKE TO REMEMBER

By Jean R. Moore

The winter months
bring joy to me
from the feathery snow
that glides on a tree.
The beautiful scenes
I would like to remember
on a pillowly dream
in blue-white December.

The whispering wind
sweeps the sleeping floor,
ice wraps the lake
from shore to shore.
So please let it stay
in my dreams of tomorrow,
let it stay in my mind
for the future to borrow.

MIGHTY SEA

By Jean R. Moore

I set my sail in the morning dawn
And the wind will blow on a reckless sea.
On a wild sea, I am sent away.
The sail thralls hushed and free.

My dory moves through breakers tall
And my sail glides on a breath of air.
Little waves lap against my vessel,
And the silver sea will whisper there.

The sea is mighty, free and bold,
On her, I will sail far and wide.
I seem to fly in a homemade dory,
Across the sea in a giant stride.

The lonely sea seems to steal,
My thoughts, my acts and the way I feel.
The sea will thrill my heart to song...
For now, I feel, I really belong!

PROMISED

By Jean R. Moore

The waterfall
is tripping gracefully
upon the rocks
below her tethered crags,
And endless are the hours
that her veil
showers love
and life
to all the earth.

The ceaseless swirl
of foam upon the sea,
prevents the bride
from ever wandering free.
Promised life and breath
is spread in all the earth
from the font of water,
springs the wonder
of perpetual birth.

RADIANT SUN

By Jean R. Moore

Over mountain peaks the sun will rise,
Casting his face over peaceful skies.
The sun destroys the starry night,
And brings to all
His glorious light.
The golden sun, the earth will fill.
And in this splendor, my heart will thrill.
Behind the clouds
The sun is screened,
But from the shadows
He still beams
Across the sky the sun will glide,
Upon the wind,
He will skip and ride.
He hangs low
On an evening sky,
I watch with awe,
And have to sigh.
Behind the hills the sun will melt,
The cool breeze
Can then be felt.

ROSES

By Jean R. Moore

Roses
make a joyful heart,
with questions
how and why;
with all the thoughts
of love unborn,
and ending with
A sigh.

Roses,
new and fresh abloom
a symbol of the pure;
a wish of love eternally,
and the greatness
of "for sure"

Roses
touch the deepest love
and all the thoughts of joy;
and everything within the heart,
that goodness can employ.

Roses
say a lot of things
that cannot
be said
with words.
They whisper
many lovely things,
that ears
have never heard!

RUSHING DIAMONDS

By Jean R. Moore

Water comes from crystal snow,
    And runs to streams far below.
It continues night and day,
    The streams will ever go their way.
Without the morning light of dawn,
    You can't see; the stream is gone.
And then once more the sun rays light,
    Reveals the bubbling stream to sight.
She keeps on running far and wide,
    Until two streams may collide.
The rushing diamonds run all day,
    In and out of rocks they sway.
She falls in emerald lakes of green,
    And there her diamonds can all be seen.
Trees beside the sparkling lake,
    Will scenes of peace and softness make.
The lake will then release their dreams
    Into many other larger streams.
Then the streams a river form,
    The mountainside she will adorn.
The river makes one mighty force,
    What is in her way will go that course.
The river can long journeys take,
    Before the destiny, they make.

The mighty force makes many turns
  Into the rocks, she creeps and burns.
Down the slope the river calls
  Tripping over wedding falls.
Into a sea the water flows,
  And returns again to crystal snow.
Mountain peaks reach to the sky
  Where diamond snow will float and fly.
Then the stream begins again,
  To lakes and seas, she will descend.
The beauty here will never cease,
  And her life-bred water, she will lease.

SUNSET

By Jean R. Moore

I spoke to the sunset
As it hesitantly
Melted on the distant
Blue mountains.
I asked all the mixed up questions
In my troubled heart.
The copper rays
Glared back at me
Like the hope
Of faith and truth.
But it could not answer anything
Of love or life or pain.
Then quickly it was gone,
But the image will remain.

TALL AND GRAND

By Jean R. Moore

I love the mountains, tall and grand,
Firm and strong as a giant man.
They tower their peaks in the cool, crisp air,
Calling on God, wishing He were there.

I love their silver bands of snow,
I love the sweet soft winds that blow.
And in her snowy peaks I see,
Many things I would like to be.

Down the slopes the water runs,
On the hills, the radiant sun.
I love the chasms deep and dark,
For in this splendor, God has made His mark.

In these mountains, I see my duty,
All displayed in their great beauty.
And there upon the grassy slopes,
Lie many dreams and future hopes.

Now within these hills of treasure,
I feel my soul fill up with pleasure.
Let God who made them smile on me,
So I can sow what I want to be.

WINTER WHISPERS

By Jean Moore 3/2017

The trees stood bony and naked of green
But the feathers of frost,
Clothed them in a delicate sheen.
The pond was a rock pressed solid and firm
No ripple or sound
From the water discern.
The waterfalls too, were one with the cliff,
Their babbling voice,
Now silent and stiff.
The pines were flocked in a blanket of white
As sentinels they stood
Stately and quiet.
Winter is whispered as nature sleeps,
Until the warm breath of spring,
Will into crevices creep.
Eventually!

OBEDIENCE

BE YE PREPARED

By Jean Moore 1-7-03

If ye are prepared,

the world is good;
trials and hardships
turn out as they should.

No matter the road,
the setbacks and snares,
it can't stop the progress
of one who prepares!

Be faithful to council,
not fearful or scared,
as prophets have warned us;
BE YE PREPARED!!

CALLED IT BLEST

1998

A marvelous gift is given to us,
For which most are wholly unaware.
The gift is a special day in seven;
A day of devotion and prayer.

But the gift is only realized
If one takes the time to pray;
Time to ponder, read and worship
On this, once in seven, hallowed day.

The Sabbath is a holy Day
God decreed it so;
To reflect, renew, rejoice and rest,
For God Himself has called it blest.

COVENANT BLESSINGS

By Jean Moore (10- 2001)

A covenant is a contract
Made between us and God.
He will bless our lives with joy and light,
If we live His law,
And do what is right.

His promise is sure;
His covenant firm.
He is bound by His word,
If we choose to obey.
But we have no promise
And are left to ourselves,
When we choose to not follow,
His laws and His way.

HONESTLY ....JUST THAT LITTLE THING...

By Jean Moore

You know it's just the little things
that cause us so much grief;
It's just the little tiny sins,
Which brand us as a thief.

The pencil that we took last week,
Or the candy that caught our eye,
Will soon evolve itself you see
Into a much, much bigger lie.

I'll never do it again, you say,
But only just this time,
I'll never be a thief you know,
…it's only worth a dime!

But can't you see, my little friend,
They "all" start out that way?
They didn't know how easy it was
For them to go astray.

Just a little thing, they said to me
Has kept me from His throne;
Honesty…just that little thing,
Has kept me from His home.

MAYBE IT'S NEAR

By Jean R. Moore

Like a giant pendulum hung from the stars
Ever so free, but locked behind bars.
With only a string, to bear the great weight,
That could snap any moment, and to all bring her fate.

No, the time is not clear, when the pendulum slows,
It may be today, that'll stop the long flow;
Or it may be tomorrow when the pendulum snaps,
Or maybe till next year; it may hold, perhaps.

We really don't know;
When the calling is here.
But prepare for it now,
For maybe it's near!

MORE PURITY GIVE ME

By Jean R. Moore
(Sept. 1995)

When we are like the fallen snow
Clean and soft, new and pure;
Then God will whisper to our soul
His message soft, and sweet and sure.
But when our thoughts and actions stray…
To paths of sin and deeds of wrong,
Then too, His Spirit flees away
And we like slush are trampled on.

If we would walk the path of light
And bask in love and heaven's sight;
Then we must have integrity
And live our lives in purity.
Oh that I could grow to be
More like freshly fallen snow;
More clean and pure in thought and deed,
More like the God I hope to know.

MUCH IS REQUIRED

By Jean R. Moore

To each of us was given a gift,
A talent unique and sure;
To bless the earth, and every child
Coming from the Heaven's door.

Talents and gifts were given with love
For each of us to share;
To magnify, expand and search
Our stewardship and care.

To some is given the gift of love,
To others Faith or Song,
To some the gift of study or hope;
And the list goes on and on.

When we serve and expand our gift
God blesses us with more
He grants an increase in our light
From His eternal store.

Do not forsake, withdraw, ignore…
His counsel is strong and His message is sure.
"Unto whom much is given, much is required."
(D & C 82:3)
(Luke 8:18)

Matt. 13: 12
"For whosoever hath, to him shall be given, and he shall have more
abundance; but whosoever hath not, from him shall be taken away
even that [which] he hath."

OBEDIENCE

By Jean R. Moore (3/04)

When are we happy?
And why is it so?
When do we prosper?
And why does it show?

When we obey
Our path is secure.
When we are faithful
The blessings are sure!

PRACTICING HOLINESS

By Jean R. Moore 7-07

Holiness is strength
To do what is right

Augmented by faith,
And not by sight.

By keeping God's law
We learn to obey

Becoming selfless and faithful,
In every way.

While attending the Temple
Will safeguard our soul

We must be prayerful,
To make our cup full.

The LORD has commanded
To do all that we do…

With Holiness of heart
And be covenant true.

PURITY OF THOUGHT AND DEED

By Jean R. Moore 2000

Our thoughts determine what we are;
Darkest pit
Or brightest star.

Rise above the worldly jokes,
Cut off the sources that feed on filth.
Replace the images of sin and fear,
Be strong in screening the words you hear.

Refresh your heart with daily Prayer
Feast on His word with daily care.
Replenish your spirit with service to others,
And polish your soul with obedience there.

THE LOSER

By Jean R. Moore

The bell has sounded
and the race is on,
The cheater's far ahead
at the first rays of dawn.

Yes, the cheater is first
and the honest is last
Cause the cheater knows tricks
from far in the past.

But who is the loser
in this great game of life?
Who is losing the most
from the toil and strife?

The cheater had lost
before the race had begun,
And loses each day
at the setting of sun.

THE PURPOSE OF LIFE

By Jean R. Moore 1-8-08

The purpose of life….
Is not to get gain
Not to seek riches,
Nor power
Nor fame.

But rather our purpose
And future of man,
Is to truly know GOD
And experience
His plan.

THE REASON BECAUSE

By Jean R. Moore

There is a daily kind of love

that so many of us miss;

But the reason because

the spirit withdraws

is we

have forgotten

The Laws!!

TRIMMING OUR LAMP

By Jean R. Moore

The virgins were ten who waited for Him;
But their lamps began to burn dim.
Five had been wise, prepared in advance,
And kindled their lamps anew.
Five had been idle and lost their chance;
Unwary, and could not pursue.

The purpose of life, in trimming our lamp;
To prepare for the day of our Lord;
And how we must watch, and wait on His word;
Then carefully do all we have heard.

But what doeth it profit, if I idle my time?
If I am careless of that which is mine?
Then how shall I stand,
If I fail the plan…
If I wasted my errand divine?

"Watch therefore, for ye know
Neither the day nor the hour.
(D&C 133:11)

PARENTS

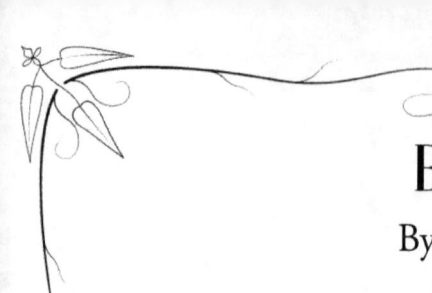

BUT I DO

By Jean R. Moore

Not all children feel
The presence of love;

Not all children learn
Of God above;

Not all children see
The rainbows of hope;

Not all children hear
The whisper of faith;

Not all children are taught
To be honest and true

Not all children have
A mother like you,

BUT I DO!!

DEAR DAD

By Jean R. Moore

Of all the people on this green earth,
I have loved you ever since birth.
You make me see the good from bad,
And make me proud that you are my dad.

I must have chosen from the start,
You must have had a place
Within my heart.
This "walk on earth" is just a trip,
From eternal progress,
That we must not skip.

There is no other I would choose,
With a dad like you,
I just can't loose.
So know that I love you on this special day,
May the blessings of God,
All come your way!

I REMEMBER

By Jean R. Moore 2-04

I remember my childhood…the memories we share
Especially, I feel, you were always there.
You would drive me to school, to friends or to play,
You always made time for me in your day.
We planted a garden and worked in the yard.
It was pleasant and joyful, though we worked very hard.

We stayed up late baking cookies for fun,
Then we'd talk and clean up till warm cookies were done.
When I lay in the hospital all broken and hurt,
You sat by my bedside, ever alert.
You endlessly read my get-well card wishes,
Soothed fears and pain with your smiles and kisses.

As I grew and matured, I remembered my youth,
You taught and explained the values of truth.
You patiently helped when I baked my first bread…
As we ate it together, my whole soul was fed.
You were there for my prom dress sewing deep into night,
Whatever I tangled, you could make it all right.

When I was performing at the mall or state fair,
You always were with me, no matter where.
When I needed help typing, or spelling it right
Your fingers were magic to my grateful delight.
I treasure the memories we have nurtured together;
As life is eternal, I shall love you forever!

MOTHER, KIND AND DEAR

By Jean R. Moore (1970's)

I love you mother kind and dear,
You always help when I'm in fear.

You are so gentle, loving and kind,
And always know what is on my mind.

Whatever I do, you help me along,
As in times of woe with your cheerful song.

The trials I face on this dangerous trail,
I know you will help me, to never fail

You are everything warm and bright,
You are to me like a heavenly light.

I will follow your example whatever I do,
In all the labors, I might pursue.

As I might stumble on life's rugged road,
You will never forsake, though you may have foretold.

In my bed, you tuck me tight
So I will stay warm and safe all night.

When I say my prayer tonight,
I will thank God for you, with all my might

I hope I have said in some small way,
The blessings you give me every day.

THERE IS A TIME

By Jean R. Moore

There is a time
Of thought and prayer;
A time of reflection
On the love we both share.

A child's love…
Is trusting and sweet;
A father's love…
Runs strong and deep.

Yet as the years
Have come and gone
How much alike
Our love has drawn!

The hours of working
And fun together,
Have sealed our trust
And love forever.

For there is a time of thoughtful prayer;
And a time of reflection on the love we both share.

RELIEF
SOCIETY

CALLED RELIEF SOCIETY

By Jean Moore

It's a joy to belong to our Father's Heavenly Throng
And to meet with our sisters and join with them in song.

We will learn to cook and sew,
and to plant and make things grow.
We will learn of scripture truths,
and the love to guide our youth.
We'll learn literature and art,
and to share with all our heart.

What is it called? RELIEF SOCIETY!
It's for you, it's for me, it's RELIEF SOCIETY!

It is for the young and old,
and the middle aged I'm told.
For the happy and the sad,
or if we're good or bad.
For each culture of the earth,
from Washington to Perth.

What is it called?
RELIEF SOCIETY.
It's for you, it's for me,
It's RELIEF SOCIETY!

CHARITY NEVER FAILETH

By Jean Moore 6/7/06

Charity requires a life time,
and is not easily attained.
It is a measure of love
And of character,
A Part of the soul
most untrained.

Real charity is not
something to give away,
but a quality of love,
shown every day!

It is compassion and healing,
Forgiving
and feeling.

It is unselfish and honest,
Unassuming
and modest.

It is seeing and doing
As Christ would do.
It's loving others as much,
As He has loved you!

CHARITY

By Jean Moore
6-1-04

Charity is a lifelong pursuit,
a goal expanding in breadth;
to be like Him in deed and in thought
is the goal of all ages,
which has always been sought.

To recognize the hand of the Lord
in nature, in others,
and in your own life;
to have patience, forgiveness,
and slowness of anger
is to exercise charity;
The Pure Love of Christ.

DISCIPLESHIP THROUGH SERVICE

By Jean Moore July 2012

_____ is an example;
A disciple of Jesus Christ;
By serving us, she is serving Him
And her Gospel light is never dim.

It might be a meal,
To help when we're ill.
It might be a hug, when we need to be still.
Watching children, a smile, or a small loaf of bread,
Is love's message delivered,
Without being said!

NOT JUST A NUMBER

By Jean Moore 9-4-09

You have never been just a number to me;
And never a burden
to visit or see.

In fact just the opposite, is true about you,
Ministering is a joy
and a pleasure to do.

Could we come in the morning, afternoon?
or at night?
We'll make the time quick,
if your schedule is tight!

I love your quick whit, your stories, and fashion
I respect your opinion,
Your insight and passion

But most of all, your testimony true,
Is a beacon to others,
in the things that you do.

REJOICE IN THE ORGANIZATION OF R.S.

By Jean R. Moore 3-2005

There is a safe place
free from anxiety
in the sisterhood of love;
the Relief Society.

Organized for our blessing
and the salvation of our souls;
lifting our families,
and strengthening goals.

In association with angels
as we hold to the rod,
it was given by revelation
and ordained of God.

TAKE NOTE

By Jean Moore

We are a people of wisdom,
For the light of the Gospel has shown;
And we must be true,
in all that we do;
The most valiant the world has known.

There is no woman so hidden,
No calling or job so remote,
No sphere so slight;
No burden so light,
That the angels of God
do not see and

TAKE NOTE!

THE PURPOSE AND PLAN

By Jean Moore 1-17

What is your purpose? And what is your plan?
To prepare for the blessing of Life Eternal,
Is the design of our being,
from before the world began.
Relief society is a spiritual work
And a temporal task as well,
In all of our doing, be coming to CHRIST;
So together, with HIM
We shall eternally dwell.

WATCHING OVER EACH OTHER

By Jean R. Moore 6/12

Watching over each other is an errand we share,
The mission; too great for one person to bear.

The Master Shepherd is depending on us,
To nourish and keep His wandering sheep.

Not always astray, but always in need,
Be prayerful and careful, in the paths that you lead.

Ministering is not a task to be done,
but a pattern of life, of what we may become.

WE ARE SISTERS IN ONE FAMILY

By Jean R. Moore 2-95
(music also by Jean)

In celestial worlds on high
we lived as family
And knew each sister as our own;
never sad nor left alone.
We are here to learn of God.
and of love and faith and joy.
If we learn our purpose and obey;
we'll return again some day.

We are Sisters and are born of God;
Sent to earth to learn.
We are sisters in one family,
for all eternity.

When dark trials of pain and sin
invade our peace and joy.
We must all recall our former love
and our sisters from above.
We must share and help each one,
to learn our Father's plan.
We must strive to gather in the fold,
our sisters lost and cold.

We are sisters and are born of God;
Sent to earth to learn.
We are sisters in one family,
for all eternity!

REPENTANCE
AND
REVELATION

BE BORN AGAIN

By Jean Moore, (high school)

BE BORN OF WATER,
and receive a pardon
from the sins you've committed, when hate has been
hardened.
He died for your weakness
that man should not perish
but live on forever, for that which they cherish.

Be faithful and strong
in the Gospel of Christ;
receive of His goodness, for He paid the price.

BE BORN OF FIRE,

And receive the Holy Ghost,
your contract is good for the heavenly host.

Let Him be your companion
through the darkest of night.

Let Him fight off your foes
when temptation is in sight.

PREPARE TO RECEIVE REVELATION

By Jean R. Moore 9/03

Prepare to receive revelation
By fasting and prayer,
by searching and care.

Prepare…by increasing your knowledge
By believing the things you can't see
By doing His will, without being told
By being the best you can be.

For when you receive revelation
It comes in a still quiet voice
…warm emotion and quick understanding;
Quiet promptings to make the right choice.

Then act on your revelation,
From your mind, to your heart, to your hands,
In this there is power and blessing;
To do as the LORD commands.

REMORSE AND REPENTANCE

By Jean R. Moore 2-21-86

(Limericks)

Have you ever been guilty of sin?
But later regretted the spin;
Remorsed for the past
Repented at last,
And began the new way with a grin?

****

Where ever you are in your life…
What ever past toil and strife,
Take count and review
Repent and renew;
Then prepare for a crown after life.

****

THAT I MAY HEAL YOU

By Jean R. Moore

In a moment of anger, I made a mistake;
In a moment of fear, I took the wrong path;
And then with remorse, I changed my way,
And sought for the Lord to forgive me that day.

Then in the stillness there seemed to speak,
a voice of peace,
of wisdom and love:

"I know of your trials, your worries and fears,
I know of your heartache,
your sorrows and tears.

For I have walked the path of life,
and I have suffered grief.
I gave my life
for you, my child
in the valley of no relief."

And then more fully I understood,
repentance is a daily path;
a divine gift of purpose and love,
requiring faith
in my Master above.

THE STILLNESS

By Jean R. Moore

Revelation

Is the

Stillness

In the whisper

Of truth

Which swells

Silently

In the heart

Of youth…

SERVICE AND TALENTS

A MISSIONARY

By Jean R. Moore

A missionary spends his nights in prayer
Seeking guidance and God's divine light.
The Lord is with him through
the hours of the day,
and abides as his shepherd
through the darkness of night.
A missionary is kind and nice to know,
Always his love, he is willing to show.
With the Gospel of Christ within his heart
he spreads HIS joy throughout the whole world.
A missionary works hard
all through his life;
His calling doesn't cease
at the end of those years.
With God by his side,
he conquers all fear;
knowing the SAVIOR
will ever be near.

AN INSTRUMENT IN THE HAND OF GOD

BY Jean Moore 1-18-07

An instrument is a tool....
of music or work or play;
Something that helps to achieve a goal
in whatever the challenge today.

A harp gives no music
unless it is plucked…
A nail, no service
until it is struck.

A ball is no fun,
unless it is played,
The clay has no shape,
until it is made.

Let us be tools
In the way that we live;
Giving something no other can give.

We each are unique,
In the part that we play,
our example, at the end of each day.

Each of us is unique to this life,
giving something no other can give.
Let us be tools; instruments of joy,
examples in the way that we live.

IN THE SERVICE OF...

By Jean R. Moore (Jan. 1984)

Service is like a bank account
...where gains and loses are paramount.
The more you invest in deeds and love,
...the higher the interest paid from above.

And if you think you haven't time,
To pursue such things so sublime;
May I remind and re-define
Service is action of love divine.

Take time to help the girl scouts
And watch your influence spread about.
Take time to be your neighbor's friend
And note how love pays dividends!

Take time to join the P.T.A.
And keep their thoughts from turning astray.
Be involved in many a cause
In keeping with God's holy laws.

When God commanded to serve our fellowmen...
I'm sure He had in mind...All of them!

"For when ye are in the service of your fellow beings,
Ye are only in the service of your God."
(Mosiah 2:17)

MISUSED

By Jean R. Moore

Each was given a job to do,
Each was given a talent to show.
He may have given more to you
To lift your friends who might be low.

Who are these friends you were to lift?
Who needs your wisdom
to heighten their own?
People must share the dimmest of gifts,
To raise their friends
To the mansion of home.

From the records of love,
Your trial recorded
Results of your gift,
Carefully reported.
Your life has been read, summed and sorted,
And your chance is gone, correct or distorted.

SERVICE

By Jean R. Moore

The Reward of Service

is the

Blessing of love

from the

Creations

of an

Eternal God.

SPREADING SEEDS

By Jean R. Moore
(high school seminary)

In the morning of life
We're all spiritually good;
But later in life,
Some of us fall,
And don't do exactly
Just what we should.
In the life of a man
Reflecting great deeds,
We find an example;
That plants great seeds.

These seeds may sprout,
Blossom and grow,
Until one day
They're spreading their deeds,
For the world to gather, prosper and sow.

To you my friend we owe great thanks,
For you have sown those seeds that grow.
You've made us think, ponder and sow;
The words of truth within our soul.

THE ARTS

By Jean R. Moore

Serving is the Art of living,

Living is the Art of loving,

Loving is the Art of caring,

Caring is the Art of sharing,

Sharing is the Art of serving...

THE EARTH IS THE LORD'S

By Jean R. Moore

The earth is the Lord's
And the fullness thereof

Ours is to nurture
to care for
and love.

Thou shalt not be wasteful
Destructive
or rude…

But be prudent,
Creative
Resourceful,
and glad.

Use your gift well,
For life will be proved!

WEAK INDEED

By Jean R. Moore
(high school)

A precious gift was given to me
From the God who reigns above,
To make this world a better place
And fill its heart with love.

Although this gift is weak indeed
And though it isn't great;
It is a gift I'm bound to give
For those who may partake.

Life's golden sun sets all too soon
For those who walk on earth,
But darkness stands for just an hour
Until you feel rebirth.

I want to use this gift from God
In the most productive way
I want to feel I've done my best
For the deeds I've done today.

I write to store your hearts with love
And fill them with His grace,
Until someday we meet again
And look into His face.

YE HAVE DONE IT UNTO ME

By Jean R. Moore

The early rays of another day
Gave splendor to the dawn;
A mother opened her weary eyes,
From her sleep, so quickly gone.

Help me this day, she prayed aloud,
To share with them, all that is mine.
To give them thy words, and share in their joy,
To impart of Thy love, and Thy goodness employ.
Her prayer was answered in every hour,
Each meal prepared with tender care,
Each talent arranged with thoughtful prayer,
The sick were blessed with spirit and love
The music combined with angels above.

That night as she prayed in her room alone,
And pondered events of the day,
A whispering came to answer her plea;

"Inasmuch as ye have done it unto one of the
least of these my brethren,
Ye Have Done it Unto Me."
(Matt. 25:45)

YOUR SLEEP IS NO MORE

By Jean Moore (high school?)

My heart is angry
with people like you,
who hide their talents
and character too!

So wake up my friend,
your sleep is no more,
and listen to the wrath
that I have in store.

Awake from your dreams
take courage at once,
You have a lot to give,
I have a hunch.
Be kind to your friends
be helpful in deed;
give a gift from your heart
when they're weary with need.

Open and spread,
the stardust of gold
that's wrapped in your heart
and needs to unfold.

Open your mind,
Open your heart,
Open that gift
God gave as your START!

TRIALS

A WALK AMONG FLOWERS

By Jean Moore 6-2022

Walking among the flowers today
I snagged my finger along the way.
Thorny roses seemed to nab and jab
At my face, skin, and clothes,
as they would grab and stab.

Roses are beauties, but handle with care,
without warning, the thorns are everywhere!
Life is a lot like roses and thorns:
Pain and surprise,
when hopes are torn.

Our walk through life, by experience stained;
Our raiment and bodies, awareness obtained.
But how can I learn, about beauty and thorns,

**If I'm only allowed,
to stroll among tulips?**

AND I WEPT

By Jean Moore 6-75

I struggled for thoughts,
but none would remain.
I stumbled for words,
but fumbled in vain.

I cried in my heart
and pleaded for peace.
I prayed with my soul
for my trial to cease.

Why am I called to this land of Spain?
I can't speak the tongue
I don't know the charlas
Why am I sent
to blunder and fail?

WHY??
.......AND I WEPT.

Then in the stillness
there seemed to speak
a voice of peace,
of wisdom and love.

"I know of your trials,
your worries and fears,
I know of your heartache,
your sorrows and tears.

For I have walked
the path of life,
And I have suffered grief.
I gave my life for you my child,
in the valley of no relief.."

OH LORD, forgive,
I whispered aloud;
and I wept.

I AM NOT TROUBLED

By Jean Moore 8-05

This life is a test
with both sunshine and rain
So I am not troubled
at heartaches and pain
I rejoice in the knowledge
of the course God has planned
I am not troubled
for I understand

I CAN ONLY SEE YESTERDAY

By Jean R. Moore

Yesterday I looked at tomorrow
I created my vision,
I dreamed my horizon,
But they melted away
At the rising of sun.

For no one can see
The life of truth,
No one can touch
The vision of youth.

No one can feel
The joy of sorrow,
No one can know
The bloom of tomorrow.

The morning arose in the splendor of gold,
But I knew it not, for I had grown old.
Tomorrow shall come
And bring what it may…
I'll conquer my dreams
In the dawn of a new day!

I NEED NOT FEAR

By Jean R. Moore

The clouds of sin are waiting by

For me to falter in the path of God.

There they stand, watching, hoping

That I will falter, fail and die!

I detest in my heart, with bitter contempt

Their shadows of evil hunting my mind.

I turn to God in times like these

In hopes of courage, I might find.

The shield of "Right" is my defense,

The spirit of God is as my song.

I need not fear with this in mind,

For I can conquer any wrong!

I WISH I HAD ALL THE ANSWERS

By Jean R. Moore (high school)

I wish I had all the answers.
…wish I had all the pieces,
…wish I had one big thesis,
…to this mixed up world.

How does one answer a question?
How does one comfort the lonely?
How does one see goodness only?
…wish I had all the answers.

How does one touch all the blessings?
How does one feel all the love?
How does one find the God up above?
…wish I had all the answers.

…wish I had all the answers,
…wish I had all the pieces.
…wish I had one big thesis,
…to this mixed up world.

…Wish I knew all the answers!

MORE MEEKNESS IN TRIAL

By Jean R. Moore
(2/1995)

To each of us there comes a time;

A test….
And a choice to make.
…to be bitter and wroth,
haughty and proud;
….Or to be humble and meek,
grateful and bowed.
The test may be long,
over days, years, or life;
but the promise is sure…
for those who endure!

PEACE BE WITH YOU

By Jean R. Moore

The cold fingers of fear

Spread an icy grip on my soul

But the warming light of love

Is the promise of my goal.

For the world may clamor in terror

And disaster may stand at my door;

But the inner peace of God,

Will sail me safely ashore.

www.ingramcontent.com/pod-product-compliance
Lightning Source LLC
Chambersburg PA
CBHW061732120626
46550CB00005B/1775

* 9 7 9 8 8 9 3 5 6 1 0 4 3 *